The Skeletal System

by Helen Frost

Consulting Editor: Gail Saunders-Smith, Ph.D.

Consultant: Lawrence M. Ross, M.D., Ph.D.
Member, American Association of Clinical Anatomists

Pebble Books

an imprint of Capstone Press
Mankato, Minnesota

Pebble Books are published by Capstone Press
151 Good Counsel Drive, P.O. Box 669, Mankato, Minnesota 56002
http://www.capstone-press.com

1 2 3 4 5 6 06 05 04 03 02 01

Library of Congress Cataloging-in-Publication Data
Frost, Helen, 1949–
    The skeletal system/by Helen Frost.
    p. cm.—(Human body systems)
    Includes bibliographical references and index.
    Summary: Simple text, photographs, and diagrams introduce the skeletal
system and its purpose, parts, and functions.
    ISBN 0-7368-0653-9
    1. Human skeleton—Juvenile literature. [1. Skeleton. 2. Bones.] I. Title.
II. Human body systems (Mankato, Minn.)
QM101 .F76 2001
611'.71—dc21
                                                                    00-023033

Note to Parents and Teachers

The Human Body Systems series supports national science standards for units on understanding the basic functions of the human body. This book describes the skeletal system and illustrates its purpose, parts, and functions. The photographs and diagrams support early readers in understanding the text. This book also introduces early readers to subject-specific vocabulary words, which are defined in the Words to Know section. Early readers may need assistance to read some words and to use the Table of Contents, Words to Know, Read More, Internet Sites, and Index/Word List sections of the book.

Table of Contents

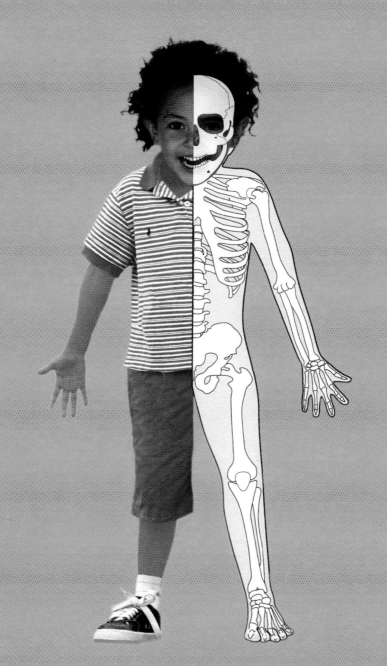

The skeletal system gives the body its shape. It protects parts inside the body. It also helps the body stand and move.

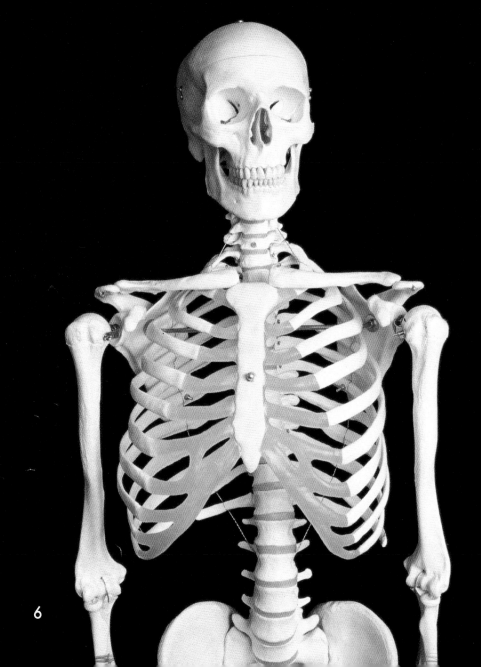

The skeleton is made of bones. Bones are hard on the outside. They are strong. Bones have hollow spaces inside. The hollow spaces make bones light.

8

Skull bones are curved. The skull protects the brain, eyes, and ears.

Rib bones are flat. They curve together to make a cage. The rib cage protects the heart, lungs, and stomach.

The spine is a row of small bones in the back. The spine protects the spinal cord.

Bones in the arms and legs are long and strong. The bones are thicker at the ends than in the middle.

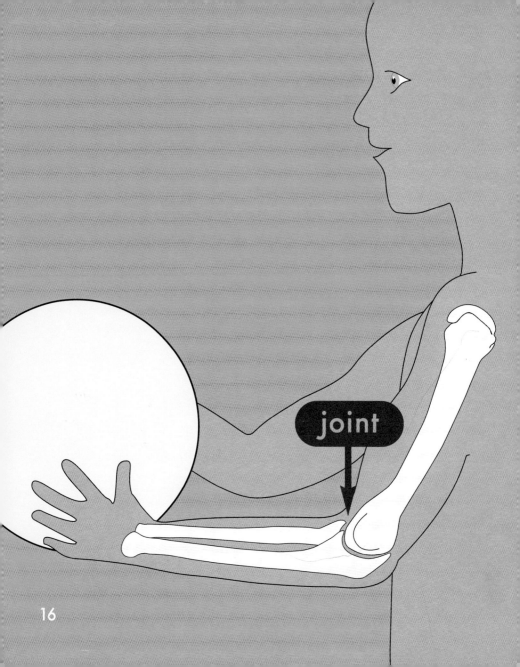

joint

Joints are the places where
bones meet. Most joints
let bones move.

joints

Hands and feet have many small bones. Each finger and each toe has several joints.

Bones are connected to each other and to muscles. Bones and muscles work together to help the body stand and move.

Words to Know

bone—a hard, white body part; an adult skeleton has 206 bones.

hollow—having nothing within; some parts of bones are empty inside.

joint—a place where two bones meet; knees and elbows are joints; some joints allow movement.

muscle—a part of the body that causes movement; muscles are attached to bones; they pull on the bones to make them move.

protect—to guard or to keep something safe from harm or injury

rib cage—the set of curved bones around the chest; the rib cage is connected to the spine.

skull—the set of bones in the head; the skull protects the brain, eyes, and ears.

spinal cord—a long, thick cord of nerve tissue; the spinal cord starts at the brain and goes down the back; the spinal cord carries signals between the brain and other parts of the body; the spine protects the spinal cord.

Read More

Ballard, Carol. *The Skeleton and Muscular System.* The Human Body. Austin, Texas: Raintree Steck-Vaughn, 1998.

Parker, Steve. *Skeleton.* Look at Your Body. Brookfield, Conn.: Copper Beech Books, 1996.

Simon, Seymour. *Bones: Our Skeletal System.* New York: Morrow Junior Books, 1998.

Internet Sites

The Big Story on Bones
http://kidshealth.org/kid/body/bones_noSW.html

Skeletal System: The Bone Zone
http://www.imcpl.lib.in.us/nov_skel.htm

Welcome to the Skeletal System
http://tqjunior.advanced.org/5777/ske1.htm

Your Gross and Cool Body—Skeletal System
http://www.yucky.com/body/index.ssf?/systems/skeletal/

Index/Word List

Word Count: 166
Early-Intervention Level: 15

Editorial Credits

Martha E. H. Rustad, editor; Kia Bielke, designer; Marilyn Moseley LaMantia,
  Graphicstock, illustrator; Katy Kudela, photo researcher

Photo Credits

David Waldorf/FPG International LLC, 18
International Stock/Michael J. Howell, 6
K. D. Dittlinger, 1
Llewellyn/Pictor, 20
Marilyn Moseley LaMantia, 4, 8, 10, 12, 14
Matt Swinden, cover

The author thanks the children's section staff at the Allen County Public Library in
Fort Wayne, Indiana, for research assistance. The author also thanks Linda
Hathaway, CFCS, Health Educator, McMillen Center for Health Education, Fort
Wayne, Indiana.

24